Steve Reich

Clapping Music

for two performers (1972)

Directions for Performance

The number of repeats is fixed at 12 repeats per bar. The duration of the piece should be approximately 5 minutes. The second performer should keep his or her downbeat where it is written, on the first beat of each measure and not on the first beat of the group of three claps, so that the downbeat always falls on a new beat of the unchanging pattern. No other accents should be made. It is for this reason that a time signature of 6/4 or 12/8 is not given — to avoid metrical accents. To begin the piece one player may set the tempo by counting quietly; "one, two, three, four, five, six".

The choice of a particular clapping sound, i.e. with cupped or flat hands, is left up to the performers. Whichever timbre is chosen, both performers should try and get the same one so that their two parts will blend to produce one overall resulting pattern.

In a hall holding 200 people or more the clapping should be amplified with either a single omni-directional microphone for both performers, or two directional microphones; one for each performer. In either case the amplification should be mixed into mono and both parts fed equally to all loudspeakers. In smaller live rooms the piece may be performed without amplification. In either case the performers should perform while standing as close to one another as possible so as to hear each other well.

Spielanleitung

Jeder Takt ist zwölfmal zu spielen. Das ganze Stück soll etwa fünf Minuten dauern. Der zweite Ausführende muß sich beim Taktieren an die Vorschrift halten, also den ersten Schlag jedem ersten Taktteil (nicht dem ersten von je drei Klatschern) zuordnen, so daß jeder erste Taktschlag mit einem neuen Schlag des gleichbleibenden Musters zusammenfällt. Andere Akzente sind nicht zu setzen. Aus diesem Grund ist auch kein Takt vorgezeichnet; doch kann einer der Ausführenden zu Beginn des Stücks durch leises Zählen von Eins bis Sechs das Tempo angeben.

Die Art des Schlaggeräusches, das heißt ob mit hohlen oder flachen Handflächen geklatscht wird, ist den Ausführenden überlassen. Diese sollen sich aber für dieselbe Art entscheiden und dabei bleiben, so daß sich die beiden Partien mischen und ein einheitlichen Ergebnis erzielt wird.

In einem Saal mit 200 oder mehr Plätzen ist der durch das Klatschen erzeugte Schall über ein gewöhnliches Mikrofon oder je ein Richtmikrofon für beide Ausführenden zu verstärken. In jedem Fall ist der verstärkte Schall beider Erzeuger mono und in gleicher Stärke über alle Lautsprecher zu übertragen. In kleineren Räumen kann auf eine Verstärkung verzichtet werden. Da wie dort sollen die Ausführenden aber so nahe wie möglich beisammen stehen, damit sie einander gut hören können.

Instructions d'exécution

Le nombre des répétitions sera de 12 par mesure. La durée de la pièce devra être d'à peu près 5 minutes. Le second interprète aura a exécuter le premier coup là où il est écrit, soit au premier temps de chaque mesure et non pas au premier coup du groupe de trois claquements, de manière que chacun des premiers coups tombe sur le premier coup du pattern inchangé. D'autres accents ne seront pas placés. C'est pour cette raison que la signature de temps 6/4 ou 12/8 n'est pas donnée, pour éviter des accents métriques. Pour entamer la pièce, un exécutant peut donner le temps en comptant tranquillement: "un, deux, trois, quatre, cinq, six".

Le choix d'une particulière sonorité [paume creuse ou aplatie] incombe aux exécutants. Cependant ceux-ci devraient se décider pour la même manière de claquer et s'en tenir à celle-ci, de sorte que les deux voix se mélangent et donnent un résultat homogène.

Dans une salle de 200 personnes ou plus, les claquements seront à amplifier, ou bien avec un seul microphone omni-directionnel pour les deux interprètes, ou bien avec un microphone directionnel pour chacun d'eux. Dans les deux cas l'amplification devrait être mono et la transmission des deux voix se faire à la même intensité par tous les haut-parleurs. Dans des salles de dimensions plus réduites, on pourra renoncer à l'amplification. Dans tous les cas les interprètes devraient être debout, aussi près que possible l'un de l'autre, pour qu'ils puissent s'entendre bien.

Steve Reich – December 1972

Clapping Music

for two performers (1972)

Steve Reich

(* 1936)

♩ = 160–184 Repeat each bar 12 times/Répétez chaque mesure 12 fois/Jeden takt zwölfmal wiederholen

Universal Edition UE 16 182

Steve Reich

in

www.**u**niversal**e**dition.com
vienna · london · new york